AF423359

Anti-Semitism and Christian Responsibility

Introduction: Church and Israel

If we truly care about the relationships between Christians and Jews, between the Church and Israel, then we are obliged to begin by facing up to how we got where we are to-day. For Christians that may well be an uncomfortable process, but that discomfort is the very least we owe to our Jewish brothers and sisters.

The very phrase 'Church *and* Israel' pinpoints the issue, for immediately it gives us the picture of two mutually exclusive entities seen side by side – whether we think of them simply as existing in parallel or as standing in contrast over against each other. Yet we know that in its origins the Church was *not* alongside Israel or over against Israel. The Church began wholly within Israel. It derives from Israel.

The New Testament gives us a picture of considerable controversy surrounding the person of Jesus. But that controversy was a family one, within the House of Israel, between Jew and Jew.

Jesus was born a Jew, living the Jewish way, observing the commandments, the feasts, the ordered prayer-life, the study of Jewish scripture. Israel was the context of his whole life. When he lifted his eyes beyond the borders of Israel and commanded his disciples to take the good news into all the world, it was to Jewish followers he was speaking. He clearly envisaged Israel as the prime agency of God's Mission to the world.

It was only in later generations that Christians began to see the Church as *over against* the Jews. The great division between Church and Israel is the original and most tragic schism which has come to divide the people of God.

Christians cannot regard the Jews as simply another people or race or nation. We cannot look on Judaism as just another religion. Whatever the Jews themselves may think of us, from the Christian point of view our faith is irrevocably bound up with them.

There is a unique relationship between the Christian Church and the Jewish people, both historical and theological. Historically, Christianity emerged out of Judaism.

To Jewish writers we owe the holy scriptures (almost all of the New Testament as well as the Old Testament). To them we owe all we know of the revelation of the one and only God. Above all the person of Jesus himself we owe to the Jewish people of whom he was born. It was from Jewish apostles and Jewish missionaries that the Gentiles first received the faith in which we stand. When we approach the Jews we are approaching the people who, under God, gave us everything we value most.

But that debt is not merely historical it is also theological. St Paul wrestles with this issue particularly in Romans, chapters 9 to 11. It is quite clear in chapter 11, verses 17 to 24 that Gentile Christians are seen not as a new growth, separate from Israel but as a branch grafted on to the original root. In other words, our Christian calling in no way replaces or displaces the Children of Abraham. Their election by God has not been abrogated or ended. On the contrary, the branch grafted onto the ancient tree still depends upon God's blessing upon the original root. Paul teaches that the Church and the Jewish people together form one people of God – tragically split from one another for the present time, but with the hope that in the purposes of God they will ultimately flourish as one for the redemption of the world.

Historical Perspective

While this is Paul's *theory* of the relationship, the subsequent *history* of Christian attitudes to the Jews is in stark and terrible contrast.

In the beginning, even after Pentecost, it is clear that the original disciples continued to live as faithful Jews. At that time Judaism already contained a variety of groups as different as Pharisees, Sadducees, and the community of the Essenes – all contending among themselves as to what was the true path of Judaism. The controversy between the followers of Jesus and the Pharisees was at first an internal controversy within Judaism, in some ways comparable to the sometimes bitter controversy in 19th century Scotland between different forms of Presbyterianism. The great dividing point began with the influx of non-Jewish converts in places like Antioch. In the book of Acts we read how the Church had to call a General Council in Jerusalem to decide the question of whether a Gentile had to become a Jew in order to be a Christian. It is significant that even up to this stage the Church had not yet made up its mind on the matter. It was not yet 'Church *and* Israel', because 'Church' was till then still *within* the House of Israel.

The Council of Jerusalem came to the decision that by being 'in Christ' the convert was thereby received into the Israel of God without further ritual requirements – and in that decision we rejoice. But what happened in later generations was that the Church became first predominantly, then overwhelmingly and finally almost exclusively Gentile. The Gentile Church then, in effect, turned the question which had concerned the Council of Jerusalem onto its head, to ask, 'Can a Jew become a Christian and still remain a Jew?' The answer that the later Church has largely given to that question has usually been in the negative – and yet the very question would have been incomprehensible to the first disciples.

The deepening division between Church and Israel was aggravated by a number of factors. First, the most fertile ground for conversion to Christianity was among those Gentiles who were attending synagogues throughout the Jewish dispersion and who were therefore potential converts to Judaism. It was only human nature that the synagogue authorities found this form of 'sheep stealing' provocative.

Then, more significant, there continued to be some *within* the Church who, despite the Council of Jerusalem, continued to argue for Gentile converts to Christianity to be required also to become Jewish proselytes by circumcision. These people *within* the Church came to be called 'Judaisers'. The ongoing bitter controversy is reflected in several of the letters of the New Testament. The foundations of Christian anti-semitism were laid when some Church leaders transferred the theological arguments aimed at the Judaising party within the Church into a poisonous antagonism against Judaism itself – and finally against the Jewish people as such.

About the time when the Church, now predominantly Gentile, was growing rapidly in numbers, chiefly among the slave population of the Roman Empire, and was thereby attracting the antagonism and suspicion of the Roman authorities, the Jews in the Holy Land launched a heroic but unsuccessful war of independence which was eventually crushed by Rome. Jerusalem was destroyed. The Temple was destroyed and the whole system of worship and priesthood associated with it was ended. The Jewish State was ended, apparently without any prospect of being restored, and the bulk of the Jewish people were driven into exile where they have remained until the events of our own lifetime.

Relations between Christians and Jews were thereby further embittered – for the Jewish-Christian minority within the Holy Land had not joined in the revolt. The Church even seemed to take satisfaction in the destruction of what it now saw as a rival religion. The Jews were simply being punished for not having given up their Judaism to become Christians.

Ever since then, the Church has very largely insisted on seeing the exile and suffering of the Jewish people as no more than their just deserts. Much *more* than that, the Church down succeeding centuries has become the prime agent in *inflicting* oppression, humiliation and persecution upon the Jews. It has also incited its members to anti-Jewish attitudes and actions, claiming that in so doing it is the agent of God's anger and hatred against those who are no longer to be considered the people of God but rather the enemies of God.

These facts may be startling and unpalatable to many Christians who are unaware of the record of Christian anti- semitism, but it is time to face them. The history of what the Church has said and done to the Jewish people, *in the name of Jesus,* is one of the darkest stains on the Church's record. It would be almost impossible to over-estimate Christian guilt in this respect.

Why Such Anti-Semitism?

The Christian Church believes that the One God, the Creator of heaven and earth, the God of Abraham, Isaac and Jacob, came to earth to be united with his own people (this most representative people), took flesh and blood and was present in the Man Jesus. Jesus was, and is for ever, a Jew. A Christian is not simply one who accepts the teaching of Jesus; not simply someone in whom the risen Jesus condescends to live by his Spirit; to be so related to Jesus is to be related to a Jew, to the most representative of all Jews, and is in some way to become Jewish, and to be related by grace and by adoption to Jesus' brothers and sisters after the flesh. The Jewish people and the Christian church belong, different though they are, to the one family of God. So – how could Christians turn against the Jews?

Some first thoughts: evil is irrational and anti-semitism being evil is altogether irrational. It cannot be understood or explained simply on the human plane. We can only discern its nature, understand what it is, see its dimensions and grasp its significance for us all, as our eyes are opened and our minds enlightened by God. Without God's word and without faith, anti-semitism remains all too frequently hidden to us like a hidden cancer in the body and because of its hiddenness, is able to flourish and exercise its evil influence over us all, growing ever more powerful until it breaks out with fearful onslaughts against God's elect people. The people who engage in anti-semitism (and but for the restraining grace of God, that can be all of us at times) are not necessarily aware of the real reasons for their irritation and anger towards the Jewish people.

Second, anti-semitism affects us all, Jews and Gentiles, without exception, for it is the expression of our natural, sinful rebellion against God and his election of Israel as the representative of the peoples of the world. The natural man does not want God and his election to salvation. He resists it and rebels against it. His rebellion takes the form of anti-semitism, which is the attempt to get rid of that means whereby God elects to salvation. In drawing us into fellowhip with God, the Holy Spirit causes us to put off the old life and to share in the new life of Christ. Yet, alas, the old life continues to exercise its evil influence over us. As Paul says, 'I do not do the good I want to do; instead I do the evil I don't want to do' (Romans 7 verse 19). We are each a 'walking civil war'. None of us can escape the influence of our old life upon us, and our old life in its rebellion against God is irritated and angry with the Jews as God's people.

Third, whereas anti-semitism affects both Gentiles and Jews, it takes a different form amongst Gentiles and Jews. Among Gentiles it takes the form of anger against Jews and all things Jewish and has resulted in the immensely tragic persecution of Jews throughout the course of history, even (and especially!) by the Christian Church. Among Jews, anti-semitism generally takes the form of assimilation, that is to say, it is the attempt by Jews to identify with a particular Gentile nation or people, to the extent that they wish to deny their Jewishness. They wish to deny that the Jews are God's covenant people and that they belong to that covenant people. It is one of the very sad facts in history, that Jews have sometimes suffered most, as in Soviet Russia, at the hands of fellow Jews. Anti-semitism can affect us all, Jews and Gentiles alike.

We cannot explain it by pointing to the faults of the Jews, for other peoples and nations have their faults and the faults of the Jews are not more than those of other people and frequently are less. Moreover, when we are angered by the faults, real or imaginary, of other people, history has shown that we frequently forgive and forget their faults, but those of the Jews which are no worse, or are even less, we continue to dwell on and exaggerate. We neither forgive nor forget. This would indicate that anti-semitism does not really have its explanation in any faults of the Jews but is something which goes deep within us all. Again, whereas there have been many acts of brutal savagery in history and also acts of genocide, yet anti-semitism is in a different category to any of these acts of savagery; anti-semitism has not just occurred at one time in history. It has occurred all through the three and a half thousand years of Jewish history. They have experienced an antagonism and hatred by other people not experienced by any other nation. Again, anti-semitism is not limited to one nation nor to one place in this world. It has been and is experienced by every nation in whose midst Jews have lived or continue to live. Anti-semitism touches us all and exerts its influence on us all, and there is no rational or moral argument which can overcome it.

The Bible testifies in many places that Israel is a people whom God has set apart for himself among all the other nations of the world. They are a people whom God has chosen to be his people so that in and through them he might redeem the world. History testifies to their 'apartness' throughout the whole of their history and to their continuing apartness today. Again, in choosing them to be apart, God chose them to be a 'representative people' for all the peoples of the world, so that they might, as God's servant, represent all the other peoples and nations before God; and in order that, through God's peculiar identification with Israel, through his presence in their midst and through all that he has said and done to them, they might represent God to the world. The very fact that, in terms of God's calling, they are representing us to God and God to us, means that when we encounter them we are encountering something deep, something real and beyond us. We are encountering God. Natural man, although not understanding the nature of this encounter, nonetheless is aware that he is encountering something which affects his inner being. He feels threatened and withdraws in irritation and anger. And his irritation and anger is in fact against God and God's election of Israel and God's way of dealing with him. However, we need God's word and the enlightenment of faith to understand this. Anti-semitism is a rejection of God and his electing grace.

How Anti-Semitism Grew

The Jews are very well aware of the record of Christian anti-semitism. And yet seldom will you hear a Jew lay the charges to a Christian's face. Perhaps they have endured enough and learned enough to know that guilt only strikes home to the heart when a man is prepared to accuse himself. Let Christians then look at the record for themselves. Let us look at the language used by Church leaders from very early times. In the second century (within a hundred years of Jesus himself) one of the revered fathers of the Christian Church, Justin Martyr, wrote of the pious hope that – 'the country of the Jews be reduced to a desert and their towns consumed by flames, and that no Jew be ever able to go to Jerusalem'.

The campaign of hatred was fuelled by often repeated accusations that the Jews *as an entire race* must forever bear collective guilt for the crucifixion of Jesus. Verses from the New Testament like 'His blood be on us and on our children' (Matthew 27 verse 25) were seized on to justify the charge of 'Christ Killer' upon every Jew. St Augustine taught that the truly representative Jew is Judas Iscariot. The golden tongued Chrysostom, famous for the crowds he drew to hear his preaching, made a special target of the Jews and of Judaism. He declared them as a race to be the enemies of God. 'God hates them – and I hate them too!' His words still smoke like acid on the pages of history, but the Church canonised him as a saint.

Right down from the early Christian fathers through the Middle Ages all kinds of accusations have been made and believed which could only have had currency in an atmosphere of ignorance and bigotry fostered by Christian paranoia about the Jews.

Jews were accused, quite seriously, of re-enacting the crucifixion with children stolen from Christian parents. Jews were said to use Christian blood in celebrating the Passover. Jews were held responsible for disease and the outbreak of epidemics. They were believed to have poisoned the wells of Christians. Looked at today, such lies seem pathetic and even laughable but the consequences for the beleaguered Jewish minorities were real and grim.

Most Jewish scholars trace the real ordeal of anti-semitism to the conversion of the Roman Emperor Constantine to Christianity. From that time the Christian Church became the official religion of the Empire and the by then fixed antipathy of Christianity to Judaism escalated into official persecution in the name of religion.

New Testament – New Israel?

The Church by now took the line (which some Christians still insist on) that the Christian Gentiles had quite *replaced* the Jews as the people of God. The Church was the new Israel. The old Israel was finished. Their special place in the gracious purposes of God was no more. The Jews were now a cast-off scapegoat race with an obsolete religion. Judaism was a dead faith, arid, fruitless, unspiritual – an affront to the true religion and to God.

The very fact that the Jews were still around; that their religion did *not* die with the destruction of the Temple; that they continued to produce great scholars and spiritual leaders, and that their faith continued to sustain them even in the face of all persecution – this in itself was a provocation, a challenge, an insult to the claims and dignities of the state religion and those who proclaimed it.

One of the most atrocious aspects of all this was the way in which the New Testament itself was used, or rather abused, to justify anti-semitic attitudes. In studying the subject, it was shocking to discover that many Jewish scholars who have studied the New Testament have declared that in parts it is anti-semitic. How, we asked, could a book written by Jews about Jesus and largely for Jews possibly be anti-semitic? But having looked at some of the things that actually were done by Christians to Jews and the use made by the Church of the New Testament to justify it, we then went back to the Scriptures. Reading them now as if our Jewish friends were sitting with us listening to the words we began to realise how chilling certain passages could sound to Jewish ears.

For example, in John Chapter 8 verses 39-44 in a conversation between Jesus and some opponents, Jesus is reported to have said of them 'You are of your father, the Devil'. This is one Jew arguing with other Jews and, in the heat of argument, using the language of the hyperbole. Nevertheless it is the kind of remark which anti-semitic Christians have seized on to justify their defamation of the whole Jewish race as agents of the devil.

A modern Christian Bishop, himself a Jew, Hugh Montefiore, Anglican Bishop of Birmingham, has remarked on the poison with which Christian anti-semitism has retroactively tainted even the words of Jesus himself – so that we cannot hear them without being conscious of what Christians have read into them over the years.

The whole Gospel of John is full of potential barbs simply because John chooses to refer to the opponents of Jesus as 'the Jews'. By this phrase John could only have meant those particular Jews with whom Jesus was in controversy. John's phrase 'the Jews' referred to what we might call in our modern society 'the establishment' or 'the hierarchy'. Similarly, we may talk about 'the Americans', meaning the White House or the CIA, or 'the Russians' when we are referring to the Kremlin.

St John, who was himself a Jew, understood what he meant by 'the Jews' but for us there is a need to explain very clearly what he did *not* mean. Otherwise we can allow the impression to get across of a wholesale condemnation of the entire Jewish nation and race.

What the Church has *made* of the New Testament in its relations with the Jews has, it seems to us, poisoned the very wells of God which were meant for the refreshment of his people. In this sense it is the Church, it is the Christians who have made it almost impossible for Jews to see Jesus, hidden from them as he is by the cruel mask of Christian anti-semitism.

In his earlier period Martin Luther began by advising the Church to be nicer to the Jews. Show them a kind face. With kindness presumably they will see the error of their ways and become Christian. But when it didn't work out that way Luther, for all his greatness in other respects, became a Jew-baiter. In his later writing, he referred to the Jews as 'a damned, rejected race. Their synagogues should be set on fire, likewise their homes in order that God may see that we are Christians and have not tolerated their lying, cursing or blaspheming'.

The influence of such words can not be over estimated in preparing the way for terrible suffering inflicted on Jewish people. Violent words breed violent deeds. Words of hatred may bear the fruits of murder, and sometimes do.

Jews living in Western Europe under the intolerance of both German

Catholics and Protestants and those in Eastern Europe under the Russian Orthodox have had good reason to associate the Christian Church with intolerance and persecution.

Scotland Also

We in Scotland may be tempted to congratulate ourselves that we have escaped the stain of anti-semitism. It might of course be pointed out that we have lacked opportunity; for the Jewish community in Scotland is so small that many Scots outside the cities have little or no contact with Jewish people. Nevertheless we are perhaps not so free of guilt as we like to think.

Even within the Kirk there is a fair amount of 'dismissive anti-semitism'. That is, we tend (without deliberate malice) to dismiss the Jews to the dustbin of history. In Sunday School we were taught to think of the Jews as people who lived long ago. We picture them in clothes of the Biblical period as though history for them stopped at that point. They had a religion which was very good as far as it went – which was just as far as preparing the way for the arrival of Christianity. Any Jews still around are a kind of relic – an interesting bit of ancient history that has somehow survived beyond its time. That attitude may not be malicious but it is still pretty devastating. How much is said today in Sunday Schools or in theological colleges about the Jews or Judaism as a lively people and faith, contemporary with ourselves? How ready are we to face up to the lively and perhaps awkward theological issues which are thereby raised for us?

In how many pulpits do we still hear unthinking insensitive remarks about Judaism in negative terms – as a dead sea, a barren field, a withered root? How often do we still hear the New Testament expounded to the detriment and disparagement of the Judaism of Jesus' day? How glibly we pass over the fact that it was the religion which Jesus practised and on which he nourished his spirit. We seem to think that by putting down Judaism we somehow enhance the Christian faith in comparison.

A few years ago the Scottish Churches Council put out a Holy Week leaflet with a comment that the Jewish way of life had become 'sterile, inhibiting, deadly'. At one time one might have skipped through the sentence without a blink. But today as we read, we have at our elbow and our conscience the Jewish friends with whom we have been in dialogue. These are men and women who are truly gracious, deep-thinking, reverend, pious, who know what it means to do justly, love mercy and walk humbly with God. Their spiritual life is *not* sterile; their ways are *not* deadly. There are areas of belief on which we openly and profoundly disagree, particularly regarding the person of Jesus. Yet whether they know it or not they have helped us to see Jesus and to think about the Scriptures in ways we never did before.

The Holocaust

But if anything has opened Christian eyes to the ultimate evil of anti-semitism it is the tragedy of the Holocaust. For the Jews it posed a terrible problem of suffering and grief. But for *us* it poses a searching moral question to our Western European Christian conscience. How could such a thing have happened in our Continent which has been under the dominance and tutelage of the Christian Church for over a thousand years? Sadly the answer must be that the Christian Church has more than a little to answer for in preparing the way for the Holocaust.

Of course it was carried out by Nazis whose creed was fundamentally opposed to the gospel. But it was Christian inspired prejudice against the Jews that made many people so utterly vulnerable to the propaganda of Hitler. According to Jacob Jocz, author of *Jesus and the Jews after Auschwitz* both Protestant and Roman Catholic Churches in Germany emerged from the War with a crushing sense of guilt. In October, 1945 the Lutheran Church of Germany made a public confession of guilt for its failure to act more courageously in defence of the persecuted Jews. There were, of course, honourable and heroic exceptions but they were pitifully few.

The Church in Poland and the Ukraine and elsewhere equally stood by unprotesting at the prosecution to its final limit of an anti-semitism fostered by the Church itself for hundreds of years. Even among the Allies the Churches emerged with a nagging conscience regarding the fate of European Jews. Protests were made, pious noises were emitted, resolutions and deliverances passed – but what was *done* was pitifully little and tragically late. The role of the British Foreign Office in spurning pleas for help to bomb the railways leading to the biggest death camps, and even during the Holocaust continuing actively to block the flight of Jewish refugees from Eastern Europe lest their arrival in Palestine should embarrass us with our Arab allies – these have been well documented. In a country which until recently regarded itself as Christian there is little cause for comfort, and much for embarrassment and shame on the part of Christians.

When Christians look at the Cross of Jesus we believe we see in it the stark consequences of our human sin. Now the Holocaust has made Western men and women face up to the horrific consequences of anti-semitism in Christian Europe. *This* is where the attitudes and prejudices cultivated by Christendom have ultimately led. Until Christians are willing to face up to that seriously and seek from God the grace of repentance there can be no real meeting between Christians and Jews. Perhaps the Saviour who from his own Cross could pray 'Father forgive them, for they know not what they do' will somehow give *us* grace to pray from the heart, 'Father forgive us – for now at last we know what we have done to you and to your people'.

Repentance and Responsibility

There is much to think about, much to pray about and a lot of humble listening for Christians to do. Any suggestion that we speak down to the Jewish people from a greater moral and spiritual height is *worse* than impertinence. That would be equivalent of the lion lecturing the lamb on the virtues of vegetarianism!

Only by genuine dialogue, listening and seeking to understand without condescension or prejudice how they walk with God, can we obey the commandment not to bear false witness against our neighbour.

Christians are committed by Jesus himself to witness to him. But the nature of our witness is crucial. When by the grace of God the Church is itself being true to Christ by the way she lives, prays and worships, when we truly walk in humility with God, and with others whom we have wronged; when the Church has really repented of the wicked distortions by which we have masked the face of Jesus from his own people – then Christ himself can be his own witness. But the truth is not served by arrogance. There must be no spiritual pride; no seeking to take the power of conversion into our own hands in imposing upon others what they do not want. There must be no resentment because of disagreement; no riding roughshod over another's faith or non-faith.

There must be such faith in God that we can trust Him to lead each of us through the faithful, humble witness of the other into an even fuller understanding of His truth in His way.

Pray God, therefore, that Jew and Christian, each in faithfulness to our calling under God may at last come to that unity of love and unity in the truth that flows from the unity of the One God whom we both worship. For Christians, that prayer is made in the name of him to whom we look in faith as the hope of Israel and of the World.

APPENDIX

The Causes of Anti-Semitism

1 Man's primary, basic sin, portrayed in the story of Adam and Eve in the Garden of Eden, is the desire to be like God, to be equal with God, to be lord of creation and master of his own destiny. His sin is the refusal to acknowledge that God alone is God, the creator of the universe and Lord of life and being. The very presence of the Jewish people recalls us to their own history, to the way in which God in his purpose for the world's redemption has set them apart, to the way in which God has made himself known to them, and through them to the world, as the living and true God. Their presence reminds us that we are not God, that we are creatures and that there is a living Lord and God who holds us, together with the whole world, and our destiny, in his hands. Against this, natural sinful man rebels. He wants to get rid of God and be master of his own destiny, but he cannot. So he wants to be rid of this visible reminder of God in the form of the Jewish people, in the vain and foolish hope that if he is rid of them, he will be master of his own fate (cf. Nazi, Soviet and Islamic speeches and writings). Again, nations and governments often act as if God were very distant and not concerned with how they behave. The Jews, however, by their presence, by their sacred traditions and by the things that have happened to them in their long history (and in our generation by the fact of their return to the Promised Land) remind the nations that God is the God of history, that we encounter Him in the drama of everyday affairs, and as nations must give account to Him. Against this, however, the nations rebel. They do not wish to encounter God and give account to Him. They close their eyes to what God is doing in history and vent all their frustration and anger against the Covenant People who are God's servant for the saving of the nations.

2 In so far as the Jews represent us before God, so in them as in a mirror which magnifies, we see ourselves as we really are before God. They are not better or worse than ourselves, only in them we see who and what we all are before God. We see how good we are. In the Jewish people, as in a mirror, we see the best and the noblest in the human race. We see faith at its highest level. Also we see how bad we are, and it is the sight of how bad we are that angers us. In Israel's resistance and oppositions to God's grace, as denounced by the Jewish prophets themselves, we see everyman's resistance and opposition to God's grace. In their ancient desire to elect their own king, in place of the only true King, in their desire then and now, to control their own safety and security, to be masters of their own fate, to take to themselves the glory that belongs only to God, we see the attitude of all the governments and nations of the world, we see fundamentally natural man before God and his grace. We see ourselves, and we do not like what we see! It belongs to the peculiar mystery of God's election of Israel that everything about man and who he is and what he is, is portrayed clearly as in a mirror. This is the mystery of God's election of them to be a representative people. 'The Jew is the man

11

from whom the cloak has been torn off. The Jew stands before us as that which radically we all are. In the Jew there is revealed the primary revolt, the unbelief, the disobedience in which we all are engaged. In this sense the Jew is the most human of all men. And that is why he is not pleasing to us. That is why we want him away . . . that is why we are so critical of the Jews. That is why we make them out to be worse than they really are . . . that is why we ascribe to the Jews every possible crime. . . . Our annoyance is not really with the Jew himself. It is with the Jew because and to the extent that the Jew is a mirror in which we immediately recognise ourselves, in which all the nations recognise themselves as they are before the Judgement Seat of God. That is why we can never forgive the Jew. That is why we think we have to heap hatred and contempt upon the stranger. And obviously it is because the Jews are this mirror that they are there. The Divine Providence has arranged it.' (see Barth, *Church Dogmatics* 3.3, pp 221ff). Of course, the very presence of the Jews in themselves is not enough to reveal that to us and to the people of the world. We need the word of God to enlighten our minds. Even so, confronted as they are with the presence of the Jews in their midst, the nations of the world are deeply aware that something unpleasant and deeply annoying is being said to them, something which they do not wish to hear and so they lash out in anger against the Jews and in so doing they declare the reality of their confrontation with God and manifest their real anger and rebellion against God.

3 The actual existence of the Jews living in our midst, confronts us with a dramatic reminder that all of us live from day to day, only by the grace of God. In his grace, God has given us life and we continue to live from day to day only through his continuing grace. We have no other real support or security. As Israel can only exist and continues to exist as a people apart only through the grace of God, so all people and all of us can only live from day to day by the grace of God. By our anger with the Jews we indicate that we do not like the fact. We like our imagined earthly securities. We continue to search for them and spend our lives in seeking to acquire them. We do not like to be reminded that our only security in life from one day to the next is through God's grace. Israel, in number one of the fewest people on earth, persecuted through long centuries and through the years of her exile, driven constantly from one country to another, demonstrates that we all have no continuing city except by the grace of God. Israel demonstrates that as the Jews in Dispersion seek to return to Jerusalem as their eternal city, so we must seek that Eternal City whose builder and maker is God. Natural sinful man who wants to abandon God, to become himself a God, is infuriated and angered by the reminder. He does not like it. He cannot stand it and seeks ever and ever again to get rid of the Jew and prove his own security, which he believes that the Jews threaten, and seeks to find that security for example in the Third Reich, which he plans to last for a thousand years, or in Capitalism, or in Marxism or in Islam. But by the providence of God, the Jews whom the world has endeavoured to obliterate, continue to exist and to remind

us of God's grace and mercy, through which alone all of us exist and have our being and life.

4 The immense contribution of Judaism and of the Jewish people in almost every area of life, demonstrates to the world that without God and his grace we can do nothing. It has been demonstrated by such people as Professors A. D. Ritchie, T. F. Torrance and also by Einstein and by other Jews that modern science did not and could not have developed without the contribution of Judaism. The immense contribution of Judaism to our modern world is in part a fulfilment of God's promise to Abraham, 'I will bless you and make your name great, so that you will be a blessing ... and through you I will bless all the nations' (Genesis 12 verses 2, 3). The world in its sinful alienation from God seeks to take to itself all the glory, and claims that in its own strength and wisdom it can accomplish all things; it bitterly resents the fact that modern science and technology is dependent on the contribution of Judaism, bitterly resents the reminder that without God's grace we can do nothing. Of course, Jews being representative of us all, can take to themselves the glory of all that has been achieved and behave in a superior way. This, alas. brings persecution. But it does not deny the fact that their peculiar and immense contribution is of God. It is God's doing and a reminder that without God we can do nothing. The contribution of individual Jewish people has been immense. Almost every major scientific advance this century has been made either by a Jew or has been dependent on a Jewish contribution. They have also contributed immensely in the fields of education, psychology, sociology, economics, politics, music and entertainment. Three men – Jews – have perhaps exercised the greatest influence on everyday life in the twentieth century, namely Freud, Einstein (whose relativity theory revolutionised the entire scientific approach to the universe), and Karl Marx. To these could be added a host of others such as Niels Bohr, who laid the foundation of modern atomic science; Levi-civita, who paved the way for Einstein; Heinrich Herz, who pioneered in research on electro-magnetic waves; James Franck and Gustave Hertz, who helped to develop the quantum theory and in nuclear physics J. Robert Oppenheimer, Edward Teller and Lise Meitner. We should also add perhaps Ferdinand Cohn, father of bacteriology; Waldemar Haffkine, pioneer of innoculation against cholera and bubonic plague; August von Wasserman who determined the syphilis test; the cancer researcher Otto Warburg; Ernst Boris Chain, co-discoverer of penicillin; Selman Waxman, discoverer of streptomycin and Jonas Salk and Albert Sebin, discoverers of anti-polio serums and a host of others.

According to the 1985 edition of 'The Jewish Handbook', from 1907 to 1984, 88 Nobel Prizes were awarded to Jews (although Jews number less than $\frac{1}{2}\%$ of the world population). 25 Nobel Prizes were awarded for physics (today about a quarter of the world's top physicists are Jews), 13 for chemistry, 31 for medicine, 9 for literature, 5 for economics and 5 for peace.

In Britain, where many Jews are of comparatively recent origin and where they number less than 1% of the population, it is interesting to note the following, that of Jews there were in 1985:

14 Privy Councillors   9 Baronets
46 Peers (10 hereditary and 36 life Peers)   79 Knights
28 Members of Parliament   3 Dames
52 Fellows of the Royal Society (plus 6 Foreign Members including Prof.
      Ephraim Katzir, a former President of Israel)
23 Fellows of the British Academy (plus 2 corresponding fellows)

The world owes an immense debt to the Jews. History shows that a country where there is a sizeable population of Jews, provided that the many restrictions imposed against them are lifted or even partially lifted, can make immense strides forward in almost every realm of science, technology and culture. Jews have had fearful restrictions imposed upon them, they have been persecuted, driven penniless from one country to another and in an extraordinary short space of time, provided there is freedom for them, they will again and again far outstrip their Gentile contemporaries in every area of commerce and the professional sciences. The world in its sin resents this bitterly. It does not wish to recognise it. In its jealousy, it will invent all sorts of spurious reasons why this should not be so, and will accuse the Jews falsely, because it does not wish to acknowledge that the accomplishments of the Jew are intimately related to the Hand of God and his electing grace. (cf. Nazi writings claiming the superiority of the Aryan race, and also recent Soviet writings.) Judaism and the Jewish people loudly proclaim for all who have eyes to see and ears to hear that without God's grace we can do nothing.

NOTE

David Torrance has written the section beginning on page 3 *Why Such Anti-Semitism?* and the Appendix on page 11 *The Causes of Anti-Semitism.* The text was edited by the Reverend Jock Stein.

HANDSEL BOOKLETS ON
CHURCH AND ISRAEL

This series began when Hansie Douglas and Howard Taylor between them convinced me that Israel was far more important than I had realised. So we decided to include a booklet on Israel in our series on 'Contemporary Issues'. The idea expanded when Dr Clifford Hill encouraged me to get something published before the Jerusalem Gathering at Easter 1986 . . . and the one became four!

Finally it became clear that a special series was indicated, sustained by the double conviction (a) that God has a great and continuing purpose for the Jewish people, and (b) that the Christian Church is (in New Testament language) grafted in to Israel.

JOCK STEIN

Advent
Hannukah 1985

THE AUTHORS

Both the authors were members of a Church of Scotland working group on anti-semitism, and some of their thinking is reflected in a report by the Board of World Mission and Unity to the General Assembly of 1985. David Torrance edited *The Witness of the Jews to God* (Handsel Press, 1982).